Discovering Reli

Christianity

FOUNDATION EDITION

SUE PENNEY

Heinemann

Heinemann Educational Publishers
Halley Court, Jordan Hill, Oxford OX2 8EJ
a division of Reed Educational & Professional Publishing Ltd

OXFORD MELBOURNE AUCKLAND
JOHANNESBURG BLANTYRE GABORONE
IBADAN PORTSMOUTH NH (US) CHICAGO

Heinemann is a registered trademark of Reed Educational & Professional Publishing Ltd

Text © Sue Penney 1999
First published 1999

03 02 01 00 99
10 9 8 7 6 5 4 3 2

British Library Cataloguing in Publication Data

ISBN 0 435 30477 1

Designed and typeset by Visual Image
Illustrated by Gecko Limited. Adapted into colour by Visual Image
Cover design by Keith Shaw at Threefold Design
Printed and bound in Great Britain by Bath Colourbooks, Glasgow

Acknowledgements

The Publishers would like to thank the following for permission to reproduce copyright material:

The Lord's Prayer from the Methodist Service Book, © Trustees for Methodist Church Purposes on p.18

The publishers would like to thank the following for permission to use photographs:
The Ancient Art and Architecture Collection p. 35; Andes Press Agency pp. 7, 9 (right), 16 (both), 20, 21 (left); The Bridgeman Art Library pp. 23, 24; Paul Bryans p. 14 (right); Cambridge Evening News p. 44 (top); Circa Photo Library p. 46; CM Dixon p. 33; Keith Ellis pp. 21 (right), 42; Mary Evans Picture Library p. 34; Glasgow Museum: the St Mungo Museum of Religious Life and Art p. 27; Sally and Richard Greenhill pp. 43, 44 (below); Sonia Halliday Photographs pp. 17, 25, 30, 31; Robert Harding Picture Library p. 9 (left); J Allan Cash Photo Library pp. 6, 15, 40, 47; Network Photographers pp. 8, 36; Philip Parkhouse p. 38; Ann and Bury Peerless p. 39; Frank Spooner Pictures p. 11; Simon Warner p. 19; Zefa pp. 10, 13, 14 (left), 41.

The publishers would like to thank Andes Press Agency/Carlos Reyes for permission to reproduce the cover photograph.

The Publishers would also like to thank:
Bolsius (UK) Ltd for supplying the candle for the photograph on p. 38 and Christian Art Ltd for the advent calendar in the same photograph; Christian Aid for the Cafédirect poster on p. 37 which is from a set of posters on fair trade, 1993.

The publishers have made every effort to trace copyright holders. However, if any material has been incorrectly acknowledged we would be pleased to correct this at the earliest opportunity.

Contents

MAP: where the main religions began

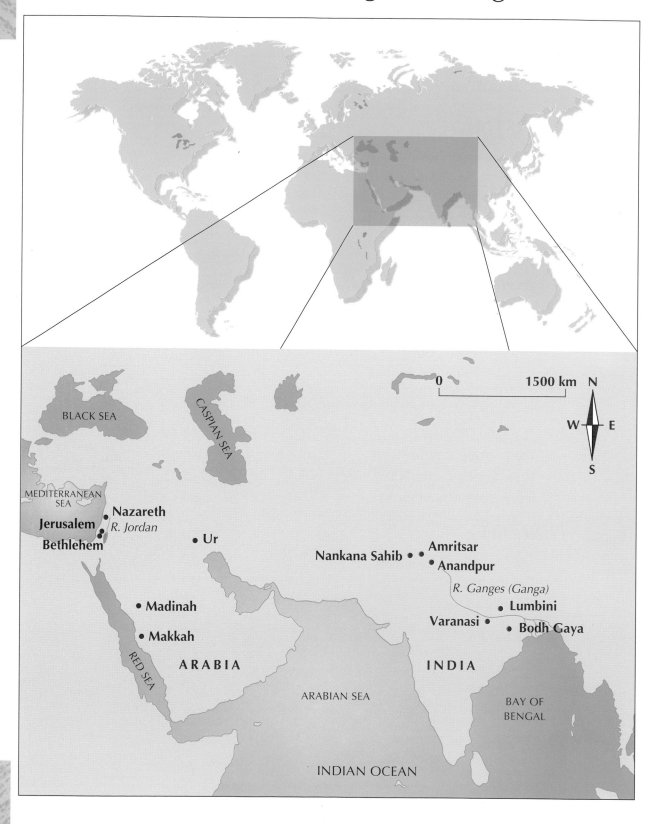

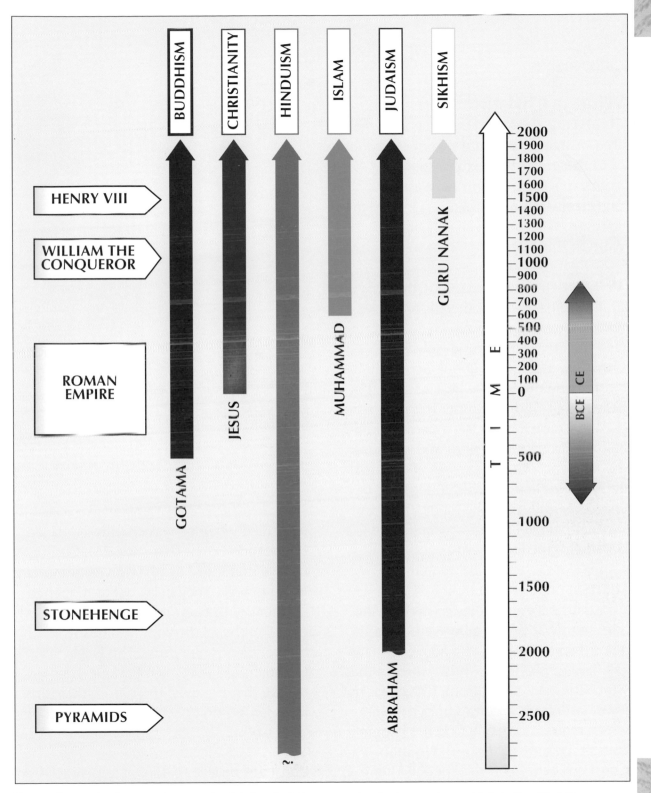

BUDDHISM · **CHRISTIANITY** · **HINDUISM** · **ISLAM** · **JUDAISM** · **SIKHISM**

HENRY VIII

WILLIAM THE CONQUEROR

GURU NANAK

ROMAN EMPIRE

JESUS

MUHAMMAD

T I M E

2000
1900
1800
1700
1600
1500
1400
1300
1200
1100
1000
900
800
700
600
500
400
300
200
100
0

CE
BCE

GOTAMA

500

1000

STONEHENGE

1500

ABRAHAM

2000

PYRAMIDS

2500

~

Note about dating systems   In this book dates are not called BC and AD which is the Christian dating system. The letters BCE and CE are used instead. BCE stands for 'Before the Common Era' and CE stands for 'Common Era'. BCE and CE can be used by people of all religions, Christians too. The year numbers are not changed.

Introducing Christianity

This section tells you something about who Christians are.

What is Christianity?

Christianity is the religion of people who are Christians. There are two main groups of Christians. Orthodox Christians live mainly in eastern countries. Western Christianity has most followers in western countries. This book is mainly about Western Christianity.

What do Christians believe?

Christians believe that there is one God, who is seen in three ways – God the Father, God the Son and God the Holy Spirit. Christians usually talk about God as 'he', but they do not believe he is a man. They believe that God is a **spirit**. This means he does not have a body like a person or an animal. He was never born and will never die. They believe that he sees and knows everything. He made everything, and he loves everything that he made. Christians say that people can know what God is like because of the life of Jesus.

Jesus

Christians believe that Jesus was God the Son. Jesus was a man who lived on earth about two thousand years ago. Christians call him Jesus **Christ**. 'Christ' is where the word Christian comes from. Christ was not Jesus' last name. It comes from a word which means 'someone God has chosen'. Using this name for Jesus shows that Christians believe he was special. They believe that he was closer to God than anyone else who has ever lived.

The cross is a symbol of Christianity

Jesus died when he was **crucified** – nailed to a wooden cross (see page 26). Christians believe that Jesus' death was very important for all people. They believe that it opened up the way to God. This way had been closed off by all the wrong things which human beings had done. This is why Christians call Jesus their Saviour. They believe that he saved them from their **sins**. Sin is wrong-doing which separates people from God.

Christians believe that Jesus came back from the dead, and is still alive. However, they do not think he still has a body like ours.

Jesus' coming back to life is called the **resurrection**. Believing in the resurrection is very important for Christians. They believe it shows that there is life after death.

Symbols which Christians use

Most religions use **symbols** to show what they believe. Christians often use the symbol of a cross. This is because Jesus died on a cross. If the cross has the figure of Jesus on it, it is called a crucifix.

Sometimes Christians use the symbol of a fish. One reason for this is because some of the first Christians were fishermen. Another reason is a sort of code. Many of the early Christians spoke the Greek language. In Greek, the word for fish spells the first letters of the words which mean 'Jesus Christ, God's son, Saviour.' So a fish is a symbol for the most important things which Christians believe.

New words

Christ God's chosen one
Crucify to kill someone by fastening them to a cross
Resurrection coming back to life
Sins wrong-doings
Spirit a being who is alive but does not have a body
Symbols things which stand for something else

Test yourself

What does crucify mean?

What is sin?

What does resurrection mean?

What is a crucifix?

What can the Greek word for fish stand for?

Think it through

1 List as many things as you can which Christians believe about God.

2 What do Christians believe happened at the resurrection? Why do they believe this was so important? How does this affect what they believe about Jesus?

3 Draw the two symbols which Christians use most often. For each one, say why Christians use it.

This altar cover shows the fish symbol

The Roman Catholic Church

This section tells you about one of the largest groups of Christians in the world today.

What is a church?

The word **church** can be used in two ways. It can mean the building where Christians meet together to **worship**. Worship includes things like praying (talking to God), singing and talking about God. It can also mean a group of Christians who worship in the same way. For example, the Roman Catholic Church. When it is used in this way, Church usually has a capital C.

The Roman Catholic Church

The Roman Catholic Church is the largest group of Christians. About half of all Christians in the world today are Roman Catholics. The leader of the Roman Catholic Church is the **Pope**.

Pope John Paul II

The Pope

Pope comes from a word that means father, so the Pope is like a father to the Church. He has a special authority. Roman Catholics believe that the Pope is especially close to God. When a Pope dies, a new Pope is chosen by the most senior men in the Church. Roman Catholics claim that the Popes can be traced back to St Peter, who was one of Jesus' first followers.

Mary, the mother of Jesus

Roman Catholics believe that Mary was special because she was the mother of Jesus. They call her the Virgin Mary and Our Lady, and often pray to her.

Saints

Roman Catholics often pray to **saints**. Saints are special people who were very close to God when they were alive (see pages 34–35). Roman Catholics believe that praying to a saint makes it more likely that their prayer will be answered. Roman Catholic churches usually have statues of the saints and of the Virgin Mary.

Roman Catholics do not worship the statues, but they believe that the statues help them to concentrate. Often, people who are praying to a saint will light a candle in front of their statue. Sometimes they use **rosary beads** to help them pray, too. A rosary is a special group of prayers. Each of the beads is a reminder of one of these prayers.

A statue of the Virgin Mary with Jesus

Rosary beads help people to pray

Priests

Only men can become Roman Catholic **priests**. They are not allowed to marry. This means they can concentrate on their work without the responsibility of a family. They are specially trained to lead worship and help people. Roman Catholics believe that the priest is the link between the people and God. A priest also hears **Confessions**. This is when people tell him all the wrong things they have done, and say they are sorry. A priest must never tell anyone what he has been told in Confession.

New words

Church a group of Christians (also the building where Christians meet)

Confessions saying what you have done wrong

Pope head of the Roman Catholic Church

Priest someone set apart to lead worship

Rosary beads string of beads used as a reminder of prayers

Saints people who were very close to God when they were alive

Worship show respect and love for God

Test yourself

What does worship mean?

Who is the leader of the Roman Catholic Church?

What do Roman Catholics call the Virgin Mary?

What are rosary beads?

What does Confession mean?

Think it through

1 What is the difference between a church and a Church?

2 Look carefully at the picture of the statue on this page. Write a few sentences to describe it. Explain why Roman Catholics feel that statues like this help them to worship.

3 Why do you think people go to the priest for Confession? What advantages and disadvantages can you think of for telling someone all the things you have done wrong?

The Orthodox Church

This section tells you about the Orthodox Churches.

Why are there different Churches?

Christianity did not begin with a complete set of beliefs. Early Christians had to work out what they believed, and how it fitted in with the beliefs they already had. For hundreds of years after Christianity began, Christians discussed and argued about the answers to important questions.

By 1000 CE, it was clear that there were two main groups of Christians. One was based in Rome, the other in Constantinople. They all shared the most important beliefs of Christianity. However, they did not agree about the answers to many of the questions that were being asked. There were particular problems over questions to do with Jesus – How was he God's son? Had he always been God's son? and so on.

At last, in 1054 CE, the two groups split apart. The Western Church, based in Rome, became the Roman Catholic Church. The Eastern Church, based in Constantinople, became the Orthodox Church. Later on, both these Churches divided again as groups split away to form other Churches. Members of the Orthodox Churches say that their beliefs are most like the beliefs of the first Christians.

Where Orthodox Christians live

There are many different Orthodox Churches. Most Orthodox Christians live in Russia and Greece, and belong to the Russian and Greek Orthodox Churches. Many thousands live in other parts of the world. There are about 500,000 Orthodox Christians living in the UK.

Inside an Orthodox Church

Orthodox churches are usually beautifully decorated. They are sometimes painted in gold. The people want the church to look beautiful to show that it is special. They want it to show how much they love God.

Inside an Orthodox church in Russia

Icons are painted by hand with great care

Orthodox Churches are divided in two by a special screen. The screen hides the **altar** from the rest of the church. The altar is a special table (see page 16). The screen has doors in it. Only the priests can go through the doors, but they are open during **services**. This is to show that there is a way to God.

Services in an Orthodox Church are led by a priest. The people stand to worship, so most Orthodox Churches do not have seats. A choir leads the singing, but there are usually no musical instruments.

Icons

Icons are an important part of worship for Orthodox Christians. They are special pictures which show Jesus, the Virgin Mary or sometimes one of the saints. Icons are beautifully and carefully painted by hand. Many icons are very old and valuable. When Orthodox Christians go into the church, they light a candle in front of one of the icons. Then they kiss the icon and make the sign of the cross. Orthodox Christians believe that looking at pictures like these helps them to worship God.

Test yourself

Where was the Western Church based?

Where was the Eastern Church based?

When did the two main groups of Christians split apart?

What is a service?

What is an icon?

Think it through

1 Using the picture opposite and the text to help you, describe what you would expect to see in an Orthodox church.

2 What does an icon show? How do Orthodox Christians use them in worship? Why are they so important?

3 Try to find out more about the Russian or Greek Orthodox Churches. Use books from your local or school library to help you. Work in groups and put your work together to form a wall display with writing and pictures.

The Protestant Churches

This section tells you about some of the Churches in Western Christianity.

What are Protestant Churches?

There are lots of different Protestant Churches all over the world. They are called Protestant because they began when people 'protested' about things that they felt were wrong with the Roman Catholic Church in the sixteenth century. The first Protestants split away from the Roman Catholic Church and began worshipping on their own. Since then, there have been many other splits. Groups of people disagreed with some of what their Church was teaching, and broke away to form a new Church. Sometimes groups have joined together to make new Churches, too.

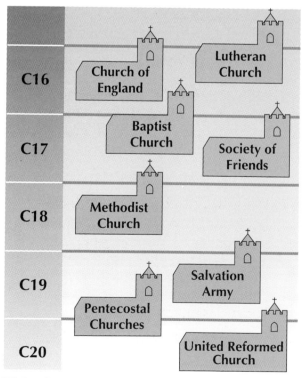

C16	Church of England / Lutheran Church
C17	Baptist Church / Society of Friends
C18	Methodist Church
C19	Pentecostal Churches / Salvation Army
C20	United Reformed Church

This shows when some Churches began (C = Century CE)

Denominations

The different branches of Christianity are called **denominations**. Some denominations have millions of members all over the world. Others have only a few members. They are all Christians. Usually the most important differences are in the way the Churches are organized and how they worship. For people who believe something strongly, even small differences may be very important.

The Anglican Church

The Anglican Church is the largest Church in the UK. In England, it is the Church of England. In Scotland, it is called the Episcopal Church. In Wales, it is called the Church in Wales. In Ireland, it is the Church of Ireland. The Church of England is the mother Church of all Anglican Churches, though they are not ruled by it.

The Church of England is 'Established'. This means it is seen as having a special part to play in how the country is run. Because of this, the Queen is the head of the Church.

Anglicans call the local area a **parish**, so churches are often called parish churches. They are usually named after a saint. For example, a church might be called 'the parish church of St Paul'. The people who lead worship are often called **vicars**. Most vicars are men, but women are now allowed to become vicars. Senior vicars are called **bishops**. The most important bishop in the Church of England is called the Archbishop of Canterbury.

A Protestant Church service

The Free Churches

Most Protestant Churches in the UK are in the group called Free Churches. This includes the Methodist, United Reformed and Baptist Churches, and the Church of Scotland. They are called 'Free' because they are not Established like the Church of England. When the Churches were beginning, this was seen as being very important. Each Church has beliefs which other Churches do not share or do not think are so important. Each Church also has its own way of worship. Some worship quietly. Some have clapping and dancing as part of the worship. The differences mean that all Christians can worship in a way they feel comfortable with.

Other groups

There are many other groups of Christians in the world. This book does not have room to mention them all. Most groups have teachings which are special to their own people. Some groups have teachings which are not accepted by the main Churches.

New words

Bishops senior vicars
Denominations branches of Christianity
Parish local area
Vicars Anglican priests

Test yourself

Why were Protestants given this name?

What is a denomination?

What is a parish?

What is a vicar?

What is a bishop?

Think it through

1 Explain why there are so many different Christian denominations in the world. Do a survey of your local area, and see how many different denominations you can find.

2 The Church of England was the first Anglican Church. Why is it called the 'mother Church' of other Anglican Churches?

3 If you were going to worship at a Christian Church, would you choose one where people worshipped quietly or one where there was clapping and dancing? Give reasons for your choice.

Church buildings 1

This section tells you about the places where Christians meet to worship.

A church is the place where Christians meet to worship. All over the world, churches are among the most beautiful and impressive buildings. They can be very large or very small. Some churches are hundreds of years old, some are new. They can even be in ordinary houses. Churches may have lots of decoration, or none at all. Even buildings of the same denomination can be quite different. This unit concentrates on the sort of church you are most likely to see in Britain.

Cathedrals

The most important Roman Catholic, Orthodox and Anglican churches are called cathedrals. *Cathedra* is the name for the throne where a bishop sits, so every cathedral is a bishop's church. Many cathedrals are very old. They are often built of stone, with heavy wooden doors. Beautiful decorations may be carved into the stone.

The shape of a church

Many churches and cathedrals are built in the shape of a cross, because Jesus died on a cross. Orthodox churches are often square. Some modern churches are round, so that all the people worshipping can see clearly.

Many churches have part of the building which is higher than the rest. If this is square, it is called a tower. If it is pointed, it

The Roman Catholic Cathedral in Liverpool

An Orthodox church in Birmingham

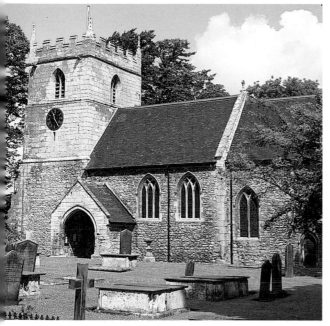

A typical Anglican parish church

New words

Cathedrals important churches
Dome roof shaped like half a ball
Spire pointed part of a church roof

Test yourself

What is a cathedral?

What is a *cathedra*?

What is a spire?

When are church bells rung?

Think it through

1 Look carefully at the photos on these pages. What can you say about the different churches? Write a few sentences about each of them, explaining the differences between them.

2 Look at all the pictures of the inside of churches in this Worship section (pages 8–21). Describe what you think makes the churches beautiful. Why do you think the builders put so much effort into their work?

3 Choose one church in your local area. If possible, arrange to go and visit it as a class. If this is not possible, find out as much as you can about it. Do a project with drawings or photographs.

is called a **spire**. Orthodox churches often have a **dome**. These things help to make the church look special.

Churches often have a clock and bells, too. A long time ago, people did not have clocks of their own. The church clock and bells told them when it was time to go to church. Today, people still ring the bells when it is time for worship. They also ring the bells at special times like weddings and funerals.

The way a church is built often tells you a lot about its history. For example, a church with thick walls and small windows is usually very old. A church with thinner, pointed windows and more decorations is usually more recent. Denominations in the Free Churches usually have buildings which are quite plain outside.

Church buildings II

This section tells you about the things you can find inside many churches.

Different groups of Christians worship in different ways, so all churches do not look the same. Some churches are very plain and simple. Others are decorated with lots of paintings and statues. The plainest churches usually belong to the group called Free Churches. The most decorated churches are usually Roman Catholic or Orthodox.

The altar

In many churches, the altar is the most important piece of furniture. This is the special table used at **Holy Communion**. It is usually at the east end of the building, which is the front of the church. An altar can be made of wood or stone. It is often covered with a cloth. It may have candles and a cross on it. In Free Churches the table is called the Communion table.

In many churches there is a rail between the table and the rest of the church. It is called the altar or communion rail. In Orthodox churches the altar is hidden by a high screen with doors in it. The screen has special pictures called icons on it.

The lectern

Most churches have a special reading desk called a lectern. A lectern is often in the shape of an eagle. It can be made of brass or wood. A Bible is kept on it, ready to read.

The font

A font is a special basin for holding water. The water is used for **baptism**, which is the special service for people joining the Church. Fonts are made of wood or stone. They are often beautifully carved.

Inside a Roman Catholic church

Fonts are often made of carved stone

A modern stained glass window

The pulpit

A pulpit is a small platform at the front of the church. It has steps up to it, and a wall or rail around It. It can be made of wood or stone. The person leading the worship stands in the pulpit to give the **sermon**. This is a special talk which teaches the people about Christianity. When the person stands in the pulpit, everyone in the church can see him or her easily.

Pews

In older churches, there are special benches for people to sit on. They are called pews. They face the altar, the most important part of the church. Orthodox churches usually have benches only around the walls because the people stand during the services.

Stained glass windows

Many churches have windows made of coloured glass. Sometimes the glass makes a pattern, sometimes it has pictures which tell a story. The windows help to make the church beautiful. Long ago, when most people could not read or write, the pictures helped them to understand the Bible stories they heard in church.

Test yourself

What is the altar?

What is the lectern?

What is the font?

What is baptism?

Think it through

1 Why might different Christians want to worship in different ways?

2 Why do you think some people find it helpful to have candles and pictures to look at while they are worshipping?

3 Why would pictures in the windows have helped people who could not read? Draw or make a stained glass window which tells a Bible story. (Pages 28–9 may help.)

New words

Baptism special service for people who are joining the Church
Holy Communion most important Christian service (see pages 20–21)
Sermon talk which teaches about religion

Christian worship

This section tells you about how Christians worship.

Christians think that worshipping God is important. Worship means thinking about God and praising him. A Christian can worship God anywhere. They do not have to be in a special place or with anyone else. However, most Christians feel that worshipping in a group is important. A meeting for worship is often called a service. Services may be held on any day of the week, but Sunday is a special day. Christians believe that Sunday is the day when Jesus rose from the dead.

The Sacraments

Some of the most important differences between Churches are in the way they celebrate the **Sacraments**. For most Christians the Sacraments are ways in which they receive special blessings from God. They are the most important services. However, different denominations do not agree about what the Sacrament services are. For example, the Roman Catholic and Orthodox Churches accept seven Sacraments. Most Protestant Churches accept only two (baptism and Holy Communion) because they believe that these can be traced back to the Bible. Some Churches do not accept any Sacraments at all, because they do not believe that God is especially present in some services.

Prayer

Christians believe that prayer is not just talking to God. They believe it means listening to him, as well. Prayer is one of the most important parts of a service. Christianity teaches that God cares about the world, like a father who loves his children. Some prayers tell God how much the people love him. Some say that they are sorry for things they have done wrong. Some prayers ask God for help. Christians believe that God listens and can answer prayers. An important prayer is called the **Lord's Prayer**. Christians believe this was a prayer which Jesus taught to his friends.

> ## The Lord's Prayer
> **Our Father in Heaven**
> **hallowed be your name,**
> **your kingdom come,**
> **your will be done,**
> **on earth as in heaven.**
> **Give us today our daily bread.**
> **Forgive us our sins**
> **as we forgive those who sin against us.**
> **Do not bring us to the time of trial**
> **but deliver us from evil**
> **For the kingdom, the power and the**
> **glory are yours**
> **now and forever.**
> **Amen.**

Music

Most services include special songs called **hymns**. Christians sing hymns as part of worship. In most churches, there is an organ or a piano. Some churches use a band or guitars and drums to help the people sing. In most Orthodox services there is a choir to lead the singing, but there are no musical instruments.

A Society of Friends meeting in Chester

Bible readings

Most services have readings from the Bible. Christians believe that reading the Bible is important. They believe that they can learn more about God by listening to the stories about Jesus and other important people in the Bible. The Bible stories can teach them lessons about how to live their own lives.

Sermon

A sermon is a special talk. It is usually given by the vicar, priest or someone else who is important in the Church. Sermons usually

New words

Hymns special songs used in worship
Lord's Prayer 'Our Father' – prayer which Christians believe Jesus taught to his friends
Sacraments a number of services in which Christians believe they are especially blessed

explain some of Jesus' teaching, and show how it has meaning for people's lives.

Different ways of worship

Different Churches worship in different ways. Some Churches use modern music and have singing and dancing as part of the worship. Others worship in a much quieter way. The best example of quiet worship is a Church called the Society of Friends or Quakers. At a Society of Friends meeting (they do not call them services) the people sit in silence until one of the group feels that God has given him or her something to say. These differences mean that all Christians can worship in a way that they feel is right for them.

Test yourself

When do Christians meet for worship?

What is a Sacrament?

What is a prayer?

What are hymns?

Think it through

1 Why do you think different denominations have different opinions about Sacraments?

2 Look at the descriptions of different sorts of prayer. Write a prayer which could be used in a Church service.

3 Why do Christians believe that the Bible is so important?

The Eucharist

This section tells you about an important Christian service.

The word **Eucharist** comes from a Greek word. It means to give thanks for something. In the service, Christians give thanks to God. They thank him that Jesus died. For Christians this is very important. This is because they believe that when Jesus died he opened up a way for men and women to reach God.

The Eucharist has many other names. In some Churches, it is called the service of Holy Communion. In the Roman Catholic Church, it is called Mass. It can also be called the Lord's Supper and the Breaking of Bread.

A Roman Catholic Mass (notice the wafer)

What do Christians remember in the Eucharist?

In the Eucharist service, Christians remember the last meal which Jesus ate with his friends. This was on the night before he was crucified. At this meal, Jesus gave his friends bread and wine. He said they were a sign that he was going to be killed. The bread was like his body, which was going to be 'broken' on the cross. The wine was a symbol of his blood. Jesus wanted to show his friends that his death was important.

What happens in the service?

Eucharist services begin with prayers. The people thank God for his goodness and for the fact that they can worship him in this way. Most services include the story of the Last Supper. The people repeat their beliefs about Jesus. Then everyone eats a small piece of bread and drinks a little wine. The service ends with more prayers. These thank God that the people have been able to worship him, and ask God to help them in their lives.

The bread and wine

In some Churches, the bread used in the Eucharist is ordinary bread which has had special prayers said over it. In Roman Catholic and some Anglican Churches, a special round wafer is used instead. The wine used is always red. Churches which want to avoid alcohol may use specially made wine which does not contain alcohol, or red fruit juice.

In some Churches, the wine is given to the people in one large cup called a **chalice**. In Free Churches, small glasses are often used, so that the people have one each. In Orthodox Churches, the bread and wine are given together, on a spoon.

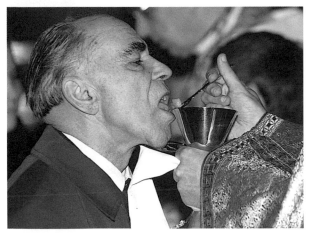

Orthodox Christians receive the bread and wine from a spoon

Why do Christians celebrate the Eucharist?

Christians believe that when Jesus gave his followers the bread and wine at the Last Supper he said 'Do this, to remember me.' When Christians celebrate the Eucharist, they feel that they are doing what Jesus told them to do. They also believe that the prayers which are said make the bread and wine more than just ordinary food. Different denominations do not agree exactly what this means.

Most Christians agree that sharing the bread and wine is a special way of sharing what they believe. To show how important they feel the service is, many Christians (especially in the Orthodox Churches) **fast** before they go to it.

An Anglican Communion service

Test yourself

What does Eucharist mean?

What other names are used for the service?

What do Christians feel they are doing in a Eucharist service?

What is a chalice?

What does fasting mean?

Think it through

1 Why might some Christians want wine without alcohol in this service?

2 Why do some Christians want to fast before they go to a Eucharist service? How do you think they feel?

3 What ways are there to remember someone who has died? What do you think is the best way? What reasons can you think of why people want to remember?

New words

Chalice special cup used in Eucharist services

Eucharist 'thanksgiving' – important Christian service

Fast go without food and drink for religious reasons

The Bible

This section tells you about the Bible. The Bible is the Christians' holy book.

The Bible library

The Bible is called a book, but really it is 66 books which have been put together. The books can be divided into two parts. The first part is called the Old Testament. The second part is called the New Testament.

The Old Testament

The Old Testament comes from the holy books of **Judaism**. Judaism is one of the oldest world religions. Jesus was a Jew, and so were his friends. The Old Testament includes many different sorts of books. There are history books, story books and poems. They show what the Jews learned about God. Christians believe that the Old Testament looks forward to the coming of Jesus, and the New Testament 'finishes' the Old Testament. Jews do not agree with this, because they believe that the Old Testament is complete in itself.

The New Testament

The first four books of the New Testament are called **Gospels**. The word Gospel comes from an old word which means 'good news'. The Gospels contain stories about Jesus. They do not contain a complete story of Jesus' life. The men who wrote the Gospels wanted to show why they thought Jesus was special. So they wrote about things that he did and things he taught. A few stories are in all the Gospels, but most are in only one or two. Each writer chose the things that he thought were most important. Much of the Gospels are about the last week of Jesus' life. This was what all the writers believed was most important. The first three Gospels (Matthew, Mark and Luke) are quite similar. John's Gospel was probably written later, and it is written in quite a different way.

The Acts of the Apostles and the letters

The rest of the New Testament contains stories about the first Christians. **Apostle** is the name given to some of the early Christian **preachers**. The Book of the Acts

The books that make up the Bible

A decorated capital letter in a handwritten Bible (15 century CE)

New words

Apostle early Christian preacher
Gospels parts of the New Testament
   which tell of the life of Jesus
Judaism religion of the Jews
Preachers people who teach others
   about religion

Test yourself

How many books are in the Bible?

What are the two parts of the Bible called?

What are the Gospels?

What is an Apostle?

Who was St Paul?

Think it through

1 What were the men who wrote the Gospels trying to show? Why do you think they called their books 'good news'?

2 Look at the example of the illustration from an old Bible on this page. Why do you think the people who did this took so much care with it?

3 Advice from St Paul's letters is still valued by Christians today. Why do you think they feel it is so important? If you had to think of a piece of advice that would still have meaning in two thousand years time, what would it be?

of the Apostles is exactly that – it is the story of the early years of Christianity. Most of the rest of the New Testament is letters written by the Apostles. Many of them were written by St Paul. He was a very important Christian preacher. His letters have been kept because they contain advice which Christians believe is still important.

How is the Bible used?

Christians believe that the Bible is the most important book which has ever been written. It helps them to understand what God is like, and it teaches them what is right and wrong. Parts of the Bible are read at most services in church. Many Christians also read it carefully on their own at home, or together in small groups. They believe that knowing what the Bible teaches is an important part of their religion.

The early life of Jesus

This section tells you about Jesus' birth and early life.

Jesus lived in the first century CE in the country called Palestine. Today we call it Israel. When Jesus was alive, Palestine was ruled by the Romans.

How do we know about Jesus?

Most of what we know about Jesus is written down in the Gospels, the first four books of the New Testament. They were written by men who knew Jesus, or had talked to people who were his friends. Jesus' name is also included in records written by the Romans.

What do we know about Jesus?

The men who wrote the Gospels were not writing a complete story of Jesus' life. Each of the Gospels includes small pieces of information. Put together, these stories tell us more. Matthew's Gospel and Luke's Gospel include Jesus' birth.

An old stained glass window showing the escape to Egypt

The birth of Jesus

Jesus' mother was called Mary. She was told by an **angel** that she was going to have a baby. The angel told her to call the baby Jesus. When it was almost time for the baby to be born, the Romans ordered that everyone in the country had to take part in a census (a count of the population). They had to go back to the place where their family came from. Mary and her husband Joseph had to go to the town of Bethlehem. This is where Jesus was born. Shepherds and wise men heard about the birth of a special baby and came to visit him.

The king of Palestine was called King Herod. He heard about the special baby, and he was frightened. Herod thought the baby might be so special that he would take over as king when he grew up. To make sure this could not happen, Herod ordered that all baby boys in Bethlehem should be killed. Mary and Joseph were warned about this in a dream. They escaped to the country called Egypt, and lived there for many years. They did not return to Palestine until after King Herod had died.

The childhood of Jesus

Not much is known about when Jesus was a child. Luke's Gospel says that when he was twelve he went to Jerusalem with Mary and Joseph for the festival of the Passover. This was an important Jewish festival. When it was time to go home, Jesus was missing. Mary and Joseph spent three days looking for him. They found him in the Temple, the

Jesus was baptized in the River Jordan

son, I am pleased with you.' There is nothing to suggest that anyone apart from Jesus saw or heard this. It probably means that Jesus was now sure about what God wanted. After he had been baptized, Jesus went to the desert for 40 days. He needed to be alone to think and pray about the work God wanted him to do.

most important building in the Jewish religion. He was talking to the leaders of the religion. Mary asked Jesus if he had not realized they would be worried about him. Jesus said 'Didn't you know I would be in my father's house?' Even as a child Jesus obviously felt that his relationship with God was special.

The baptism of Jesus

Apart from this one story, nothing else is known about Jesus until he reached the age of about 30. A man known as John the Baptist had begun teaching and baptizing Jews. As John was teaching one day, Jesus went to him and asked to be baptized. At first, John did not want to, because he said that Jesus was a much better person than he was. But Jesus insisted, and John baptized him.

Mark's Gospel says that God's Spirit came down from heaven as a dove and rested on Jesus. A voice said 'You are my own dear

New word

Angel messenger of God

Test yourself

Who ruled Palestine at the time of Jesus?

What is an angel?

What is a census?

Why did Herod order all baby boys in Bethlehem to be killed?

How does Mark say God's Spirit came down?

Think it through

1 The Gospels do not include any of the details you would expect to find in the story of someone's life. Why do you think this is so?

2 Why might Jesus have wanted to be alone to think and pray after he had been baptized?

3 Write a story (real or imagined) about something happening to you which changes the way you live.

The ministry of Jesus

This section tells you about Jesus' later life, and his death and resurrection.

Jesus' preaching

Jesus began teaching when he was about 30 years old. For about three years, he went from place to place teaching people. This is what Christians call his **ministry**. He spent most of his time in the part of northern Palestine called Galilee. He seems to have had a base in the town of Capernaum. He collected a group of friends who travelled with him. They are often called his **disciples**. His three closest disciples were Peter, James and John. There were obviously many other people who spent time with him when they could.

Palestine at the time of Jesus

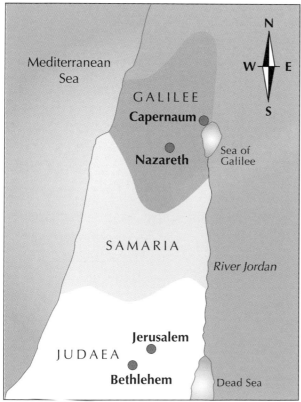

Ordinary people liked listening to Jesus. But the people who were in charge of Palestine did not like some of the things that Jesus said. They were afraid that his preaching might turn the people against them. They decided they had to get rid of Jesus. They began to look for a chance to send soldiers to arrest him. They were afraid to do this when there were crowds of people around.

Jesus is arrested

Jesus went to Jerusalem, the capital city of Palestine. It was the time of the Jewish festival of Passover. Jesus shared the Passover meal with his disciples. This was the last meal he ate with them, so Christians call it the Last Supper. During the meal, Jesus gave his disciples bread and wine. He said these were symbols of the fact that he was going to die. Then they all went to a quiet garden. There were no crowds who might fight for Jesus. Soldiers came and arrested him. The Roman Governor, a man called Pontius Pilate, ordered that Jesus should be killed.

Jesus' death

Soldiers crucified Jesus. This means they nailed him to a cross made of wood. It is one of the most cruel ways of killing someone which has ever been known. After Jesus died, his friends took his body down from the cross. They put the body in a cave and rolled a rock across the entrance. This was what usually happened in those days when people died. Everyone thought that this was the end of Jesus.

An artist's idea of Jesus' crucifixion

The resurrection

The Gospels say that two days later, early on Easter Sunday morning, two women friends of Jesus went to visit his grave to **anoint** his body. They had not been able to go before then. This was because Saturday is the Jewish Sabbath, the holy day, when carrying things is not allowed. When they got to the cave, they found that the stone had been moved. The body had gone! Two men wearing shining white clothes told them that Jesus had risen from the dead.

New words

Anoint to rub with oil
Disciples special friends of Jesus
Ministry Jesus' preaching and teaching

Christians call this the resurrection, and believe that it is very important. They believe it shows that death is not the end and that people who believe in Jesus do not need to be afraid of death. This is a very important part of Christian belief.

Even Christians who believe in the resurrection do not really understand what happened. They believe that nothing like it has happened before or since.

Test yourself

Where did Jesus do most of his preaching?

What is a disciple?

What was the Last Supper?

What does anoint mean?

What was the resurrection?

Think it through

1 Explain why the people who were in charge of the country wanted to get rid of Jesus. Why did they have to be careful how they did this?

2 Why do Christians believe that the resurrection was so important? What difference do you think believing in it makes to a Christian's life?

3 Working in groups, produce a play about what happened on Easter Sunday morning. (You'll need to include the women and the men at the tomb.)

Jesus' teaching – parables

This section tells you about two of the stories that Jesus told.

When he was teaching, Jesus often told stories to help people understand his message. Stories are interesting to listen to and they can make people think about the way they live. They can teach people lessons, too. Jesus' stories often had a meaning. A story with a meaning is called a **parable**.

One day Jesus was teaching about the right way to live. Jewish teaching said that you should 'love your neighbour as yourself'. A man from the crowd asked, 'who is my neighbour?' Jesus wanted to show the people that your neighbour is anyone who needs your help. So to answer the question he told them this story. You can find it in the Bible in Luke's Gospel, chapter 10 verses 25–37.

The Parable of the Good Samaritan

The Parable of the Good Samaritan

A Jewish man was walking from the city of Jerusalem to the town of Jericho. It was a lonely road, and he was attacked by robbers. They left him half-dead. A priest came by on his way to Jerusalem. Then a Levite walked past. (Levites were important people in the Jewish religion.) Both these important men could have helped the man who was hurt. But they only wanted to look after themselves, and they walked on. Then a Samaritan came past. He stopped and gave the man 'first aid'. He took him to an inn, and even paid for him to be looked after until he was better.

There are two lessons in this story. The two men who walked past did not want to risk touching a dead body. According to Jewish teaching, if the man had been dead and they had touched him, they would have become 'unclean'. This means far more than just being dirty. They would have had to go through special ceremonies before they were able to do their jobs in the Temple again. Jesus was criticizing people who did not make helping others the most important thing in their lives.

The other lesson of the story was in choosing a Samaritan to be its 'hero'. In those days, Samaritans and Jews hated each other. The crowd who were listening would not have expected the Samaritan to help. The lesson of the story was unpleasantly clear to them. You should help anyone who needs it, even if it is someone you do not like.

The Parable of the Sower

You will find this story in Mark's Gospel, chapter 4 verses 3–20.

A farmer went out to sow some seed. (In those days, seed was sown by hand.) As the farmer threw the seed, some fell on the path and birds ate it. Some fell on ground where there was not much soil. It could not grow deep enough for roots, and it died. Some fell in weeds. It tried to grow, but there were too many weeds, and the tiny plants died. Some seed fell on good ground. It grew well, and gave a good crop.

Jesus said that the seed was like his teaching. Some people took no notice, like the seed that was eaten. Some made a good start at following him, but soon gave up. They were like the seed with no roots. Some listened and tried to follow his teaching, but problems got in the way and they gave up. They were like the seed that fell among weeds. A few people listened, and the teaching helped them live better lives.

New word

Parable story with a special meaning

The Parable of the Sower

Test yourself

What is a parable?

Why would the crowd not expect the Samaritan to help?

How was seed sown in those days?

What did Jesus say the seed was like?

Think it through

1 Explain why Jesus taught in parables. Why do Christians today still take notice of the teachings?

2 What lessons does the Parable of the Sower teach Christians today?

3 In small groups, produce a play about the story of the Good Samaritan. How will you get the lesson of the story across?

Jesus' teaching – miracles

This section tells you about two of Jesus' **miracles**.

What is a miracle?

A miracle is something that cannot be explained. It shows a power that we cannot understand. Christians believe that Jesus had special power which came from God.

The Gospels include many stories about Jesus working miracles. He made very ill people better. He made 'impossible' things happen. The men who wrote the Gospels believed that Jesus could do these things because he was the Son of God. They wanted to show the people reading the Gospels why they believed this. So they included the miracle stories to show how Jesus used his power.

The Sea of Galilee today. Many of Jesus' miracles happened in this area

The healing of the man let down through the roof

You can find this story in Mark's Gospel, chapter 2 verses 2–12.

Jesus was preaching in a house in Capernaum one day when four men arrived carrying a friend who was paralysed. They could not get near the house because there were so many people listening to Jesus, so they climbed up on the roof. Houses in Palestine in those days were made of baked mud and had flat roofs with stairs outside.

The men made a hole in the roof big enough to let the stretcher through. When the man was let down in front of him, Jesus said 'Your sins are forgiven.' In those days, people believed that illness was often a punishment for things that a person had done wrong.

Some strict Jews who were present began to mutter to each other, asking who Jesus thought he was that he dared to forgive sins. They believed that only God had the power to do that. Jesus heard them, and asked them whether it was easier to tell the man his sins were forgiven, or to say 'Get up, pick up your mat and go home!' The man got up and walked away. All the people were amazed.

Jesus feeds five thousand people

This miracle is the only one which is found in all four Gospels. This is how Mark tells the story. (Mark 9:2–17)

A mosaic picture of the five loaves and two fish

Jesus had been teaching a large crowd of people all day. It was getting late and the disciples said that he should send the people home. Instead, Jesus told the disciples to find food for everyone. The best they could find was a boy who had a packed lunch with him. He had five bread rolls and two small fish. The disciples did not think this would be any use, but Jesus took the food and said a prayer. Then he told the disciples to give it to the people. Everyone ate as much as they wanted. When they had finished, there was enough left over to fill twelve food baskets.

Can the miracle stories be explained?

No-one really knows what happened when Jesus worked miracles. Many Christians believe that they are accounts of things that really happened and that they show God's power. Some people believe that they can be explained scientifically. Others believe that they are symbols. All Christians would agree that for the men who wrote the Gospels, the miracles were signs that Jesus was a special person.

New word

Miracles amazing events which show God's power

Test yourself

What is a miracle?

What did the Gospel writers believe the miracles showed?

Where was the house where Jesus was preaching?

Why did Jesus tell the man his sins were forgiven?

How many people did Jesus feed?

Think it through

1 Explain the reasons why the writers included miracles in their Gospels. What do Christians today believe about them?

2 Work in pairs to make up a conversation between the boy with the packed lunch and his mother when he returned home. How do they think they both felt?

3 People often talk today of miracles happening. Work in groups to make a list of things which have been described like this. Discuss whether you think any are the same sort of miracle as in the Bible.

The growth of Christianity

This section tells you about the early years of Christianity.

The beginning of a new religion

Jesus and all his first disciples were Jews. They almost certainly had no idea of starting a new religion. At first, the people who followed Jesus' teachings were Jews who believed that Jesus was special. Then little by little, things became more complicated.

Early problems

In those days, Jews tried not to have anything to do with people who were not Jews. They would not eat with anyone who was not Jewish or go into their house. They even tried not to talk to anyone who was not Jewish.

People who were not Jews heard about Jesus. They wanted to follow his teachings, too. The Christians were not sure if this could be allowed.

Peter's vision

Peter was one of the most important of the first Christians, because he had been one of Jesus' closest friends. While the discussions were going on about whether or not followers of Jesus had to be Jews, Peter had a **vision**. He saw a cloth being let down from the sky. It was full of animals and birds. A voice told Peter to kill and eat. Jews have strict laws about food which they can and cannot eat, and many of the things in the cloth were not allowed. Peter was horrified, and said that he could not possibly eat them. The voice told him that God had made them, and it was not for him to judge whether they were fit to eat or not. This happened three times.

While Peter was wondering what the vision meant, a messenger arrived from a Roman soldier called Cornelius. He was not a Jew, but he was very interested in the Jewish religion. He had had a vision telling him to ask Peter to go and teach him. Peter understood that the two visions were connected. Just as he had no right to judge

How Christianity spread

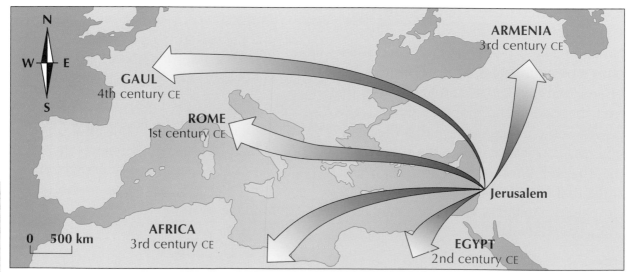

ARMENIA
3rd century CE

GAUL
4th century CE

ROME
1st century CE

Jerusalem

AFRICA
3rd century CE

EGYPT
2nd century CE

0   500 km

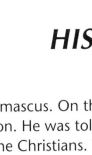

An early Christian statue of Jesus

which animals were fit to eat, he should not judge who to teach about Jesus.

There were still many discussions, but at last it was decided that non-Jews could become followers of Jesus. This was very important. It meant that the new religion of Christianity could reach far more people.

St Paul

One man was especially important in helping Christianity to spread. He was a Jew called Saul. At first, Saul was very angry when he heard what the Christians were teaching. He thought it was wrong to worship a man as they worshipped Jesus. He went to see the leaders of the Jews. They gave Saul permission to arrest as many Christians as he could find. He set off

New word

Vision dream which includes a religious experience

to a town called Damascus. On the way there, he had a vision. He was told by Jesus to stop punishing the Christians. The vision changed Saul's life completely. He became a Christian. He changed his name to Paul, and spent the rest of his life teaching people about Christianity. He was one of the most important Christian teachers who has ever lived.

Test yourself

What religion was Jesus?

Why was Peter such an important Christian?

What had Cornelius been told?

Where was Saul going when he had his vision?

What did Saul change his name to?

Think it through

1 Why do you think people who were not Jews wanted to become Christians? Why was this a complicated problem?

2 Explain carefully what happened in Peter's vision. Draw a picture to illustrate it if you wish. Why was the vision so important?

3 Find out more about St Paul's life. Books on the Bible will help. Look at some of his letters in the New Testament. Write a few sentences about what you have learned.

The Saints

This section tells you about some Christian saints.

What is a saint?

A saint is someone who lived an especially good life. They were very close to God when they were alive. Many Christians believe that because they were so good when they were alive, they are still special after their death. Some Christians, especially in the Roman Catholic and Orthodox Churches, pray to saints. They believe that the saints can help them. (Notice that saint is often written as St.)

St Francis

One of the best-loved saints is St Francis. He was born in the town of Assisi in Italy in 1181 CE. He was the son of a rich merchant, and could have had a comfortable life, but he felt that God was telling him to live in a very different way. He left home, and chose to live in great poverty. He wore only simple clothes, and lived in a mud hut with no furniture and only a few books. He spent much of his life caring for the poor and sick. He was joined by seven men who shared his view of life. From this developed the Franciscans, an **Order** of **monks** which still exists today. St Francis is remembered for how he lived, and for the way in which he saw everything in the world as being part of God's creation.

Patron saints

When they prayed to the saints, people sometimes began to believe that a particular saint was helping them. This led to the idea of saints being interested in

An old painting showing St Andrew with his cross

particular situations. Usually this is because of the job they did, or because of something that happened to them when they were alive. Saints with a special interest are called **patron saints**.

Each country has its own patron saint. The four patron saints of the British Isles are Patrick (Ireland), David (Wales), Andrew (Scotland) and George (England). Each country celebrates their saint in different ways. For example, the flag of Scotland shows St Andrew's cross, a diagonal cross on which he is said to have been crucified.

Every saint has a day on which he or she is especially remembered, and there are often special ceremonies in a country to celebrate the patron saint's day. St David's day is 1 March, St Patrick's day is 17 March, St George's day is 23 April, St Andrew's day is 30 November.

St Christopher

St Christopher is the patron saint of people who are travelling. The story says that there was a giant called Opher. His job was to help people across a river. One day a child asked to be carried across. As they crossed, the child became so heavy that Opher could hardly carry him. When they got to the other side, the child said that he was Jesus and that the weight that Opher had felt was the weight of the sins of the world. He told Opher to change his name from Opher (which means carrier) to Christopher, because he had carried Christ.

Pilgrimage

Many people think that the place where a saint lived or died is important. Sometimes they go on a special journey to visit it. This journey is called a **pilgrimage**. One of the most important places of pilgrimage in Britain is Canterbury Cathedral. This is where St Thomas à Becket was killed in 1170 CE.

New words

Monks men who dedicate their life to God

Order group of monks or nuns who live by the same rules

Patron saints saints with a special interest in a country or situation

Pilgrimage journey made for religious reasons

Test yourself

What is a saint?

What is a monk?

What is a patron saint?

Who is the patron saint of travellers?

What is a pilgrimage?

Think it through

1 What sort of a person do you think St Francis was? What made him give up his easy life?

2 What reasons might people have for going on a pilgrimage? Write a few sentences about a place that is special for you.

3 Choose one of the saints in this unit. For each one, write a brief story of their life, with a picture to show their special interest.

This tablet marks the spot where St Thomas à Becket was killed

Christianity today

This section tells you something about being a Christian today.

Christianity is the largest religion in the world. In 1997, 1700 million people had a link with Christianity. Different Christians live in different ways. Not all of them believe exactly the same things. Some Christians think that it is enough just to believe in Jesus. Other Christians believe they should give their whole life to God.

Monks and nuns

There are thousands of monks and **nuns** today. Most of them belong to the Roman Catholic or Orthodox Churches. They are ordinary men and women who have decided to live in a special way. They try to spend their whole life serving God and helping other people. Some monks and nuns help others by working with people. They often become teachers or nurses. Other monks and nuns live in 'enclosed' Orders. This means they have as little as possible to do with people outside the Order. They can spend all their time praying and **meditating**. They believe this is a way of helping the world.

Vows

All monks and nuns make special promises. These promises are called **vows**. For example, they promise that they will not marry. This means they can concentrate on their work, and they do not have to care for a family. They promise they will not own things. They are given things that they need, like clothes and food. This means they do not have to worry about money and possessions. They promise that they will follow the rules of their group. This means they do not have to think about the way they live. All these things mean they are free to think about serving God.

Helping others

Christians believe that helping other people is important. They believe that God cares about everyone in the world and that Christians should care about people, too. Some Christians spend all their time working with people who need help. Others spend some of their spare time helping other people. Some Christians give money so that people can be helped. All Christians should try to live in a way that does not harm other people.

Nuns and monks work in many different ways

Drink a fair up of coffee!

These friends drink Cafédirect happily, knowing the pickers of this coffee have decent conditions. It is the first fairly traded supermarket coffee.

Christian Aid

Small actions can help other people

New words

Meditate to think deeply, especially about religion

Missionary someone who travels to preach

Nuns women who dedicate their life to God

Vows solemn promises

Test yourself

About how many people in the world are Christian?

Which branches of Christianity do most nuns and monks belong to?

What does meditate mean?

What is a vow?

What is a missionary?

Think it through

1 What advantages and disadvantages can you think of in being a monk or nun?

2 A hundred years ago, working as a missionary was very different from how it is today. Explain what the differences are. Why do you think missionaries today have a different attitude?

3 See if it is possible to arrange for a speaker from a Christian charity to come and talk about the charity's work.

Missionaries

Some Christians believe that God wants them to help people living in other countries. Someone who travels to another country to preach is called a **missionary**. Once, missionaries went to countries just to try to persuade the people to become Christians. Today, Christians who go to other countries usually do so because they can work with the people there, for example as engineers or doctors. Many people who want to help in this way work with charities that are run by Christians, such as Christian Aid and Tearfund.

Celebrations 1

This section tells you about important events in the first part of the Christian year.

Advent

The Church year begins in December. The first season is called Advent. Advent means 'coming'. It is the name given to the four weeks before Christmas. At Christmas, Christians remember Jesus' birth. So Advent is the time when Christians look forward to Jesus' coming to earth. It is a time of hope, and a time for preparation. This does not mean buying cards and presents, though of course Christians do that too. It means thinking about why Jesus' birth was so important.

In Advent, Christians use special candles and calendars. Advent candles have marks to show the days until Christmas. The candle is lit each day until it burns down to the next mark. Advent calendars have little doors to open, one for each day. Behind each door is a picture. Candles and calendars like this help to remind people that Christmas is coming closer. They also remind people how important Christmas is.

Christmas

Christmas is the time when Christians remember and celebrate the birth of Jesus. They believe that this was very important, because Jesus is God's son.

In most parts of the world, Christmas Day is on 25 December. This was not the date Jesus was born, which no-one knows. It has been the date for celebrating Christmas since at least 300 CE. In countries where Orthodox Christians live, it is 6 January, because of the difference in calendars.

Christians usually try to go to church at Christmas. There are often special services. One of the most important is held at midnight on Christmas Eve. The services include Bible readings about Jesus' birth and special songs called **carols**. Christians thank God for giving his son Jesus to the world. Christmas is now also a holiday and a special time for many people who are not Christians.

Boxing Day

Boxing Day is on 26 December. This name goes back hundreds of years. In those days, many people were very poor. All through the year, people put money in special boxes which were kept in churches. On Boxing Day the boxes were opened and the money was given to the poor.

An Advent calendar and candle

A Christmas crib

Epiphany

In the Western Church, Epiphany is on 6 January. It is the end of the Church season of Christmas, which lasts for twelve days. Epiphany comes from a Greek word which means 'showing'. It celebrates the story in Matthew's Gospel about how Jesus was shown to the wise men who had travelled to see him following a star.

In Orthodox Churches which celebrate Christmas on 6 January, Epiphany is on 19 January. For Orthodox Christians, Epiphany is a time to celebrate when Jesus was shown to be the Son of God at his baptism (see page 25).

New word

Carols joyful songs

Test yourself

What is the first season of the Church year?

What are the two dates for celebrating Christmas?

What is a carol?

When is Boxing Day?

What does Epiphany mean?

Think it through

1 What does the name Advent mean? Why do you think Christians want to prepare so carefully for Christmas?

2 The word 'carol' once meant a dance. What does this tell you about Christmas celebrations in olden days?

3 What two things do Christians remember at Epiphany? What do they both show?

Celebrations II

This section tells you about the most important festivals for Christians.

Lent

Lent is the name for the six weeks before Easter. It is a very serious time of year for Christians. They remember when Jesus was in the desert thinking about how to do the work God wanted. Christians try to live especially good lives during Lent. The day before Lent begins is called Shrove Tuesday.

Shrove Tuesday

Shrove is a very old word. It means being forgiven for things you have done wrong. For some Christians, Shrove Tuesday is an important day for going to Confession (see page 9). It is a time for a new start before Lent. Another name for Shrove Tuesday is 'Pancake Day'. Many years ago, people used to eat very plain foods in Lent. It became the custom to eat pancakes on Shrove Tuesday, to use up rich foods like fat and eggs before Lent began. Many Christians still choose to give up something for Lent. In Orthodox Churches, Lent is still a time of strict fasting.

Ash Wednesday

The first day of Lent is called Ash Wednesday. On Ash Wednesday some Christians go to a serious church service. Special ash is put on their forehead in the shape of a cross. It is a sign that they are really sorry for things they have done wrong.

Easter

Easter is the most important Christian festival. It takes place in spring, and it is a festival of new life. Christians remember

Easter eggs are a symbol of new life

Jesus' death and his coming back to life, which is called the resurrection.

Holy Week

The week before Easter is called Holy Week. It is the time when Christians remember the important events just before Jesus' crucifixion (see page 26). It begins on Palm Sunday, when Christians remember how Jesus rode into Jerusalem on a donkey. The name comes from the palm leaves which people spread on the road in front of him.

Maundy Thursday

Maundy Thursday is the day when Jesus ate the Last Supper with his disciples. This is the meal which Christians remember in the service of the Eucharist (see pages 20–21).

Good Friday

On Good Friday, Christians remember Jesus crucifixion. Christians believe that this opened up a way to God. That is why it is called Good Friday, even though Jesus died. It is a very sad and serious day. Churches never have flowers or other decorations on Good Friday.

An Orthodox service at Easter

Easter Day

Easter Sunday is a very joyful day. Christians believe that Jesus rose from the dead on this day. They believe that this changed the world forever. They believe that he is still alive today, though not on earth and not in a human body. Many Christians make a special effort to go to a Eucharist service on Easter Day, because it is so important. Orthodox Churches have a special service that begins at midnight on Easter Saturday. The church is in darkness until the priest comes from behind the centre screen with a lighted candle. All the people light their candles from his, until the church is filled with light.

Test yourself

How long does Lent last for?

What is the first day of Lent called?

Where does the name Palm Sunday come from?

What happened on Good Friday?

What do Christians celebrate on Easter Sunday?

Think it through

1 What do Christians remember during the time of Lent? Why do many Christians choose to give up something for Lent?

2 Explain why Good Friday has this name.

3 How do you think Christians feel on Easter Sunday?

Celebrations III

This section tells you about other important Christian festivals.

Ascension Day (Acts 1:9–11)

Ascension Day is 40 days after Easter. It is the day when Christians remember the last time that Jesus' disciples saw him on earth. No-one is really sure what happened on this day. The Bible says that as Jesus left them 'a cloud hid him from their sight.' Some Christians believe that there was a miracle and Jesus was lifted up into the clouds. Other Christians believe that he walked away up the hill. The disciples knew that they were not going to see him again.

Pentecost (Acts 2:1–4)

Pentecost takes place 50 days after Easter. At Pentecost, Christians remember when the first Christians were given the Holy Spirit. Christians believe that the Holy Spirit is God's power – the way God works through people in the world. They believe

Many Christians take part in processions at Pentecost

that at Pentecost, the first Christians were given this power. The disciples were hiding in a room in Jerusalem when they heard a noise like a rushing wind and saw tongues like flames on each other's heads. They forgot they were afraid, and rushed outside. They began teaching people about Jesus.

After this, they could do the things that Jesus did, like teaching people and making ill people well. Because this was so important, many people say that Pentecost is like the birthday of Christianity. It was the day that Christianity really began.

At Pentecost, many Christians join in walks around their town or village. They want to show that they believe the Holy Spirit is still working today and helps them to live better lives. The other name for Pentecost is Whit Sunday. This goes back to the days when people often joined the Church and were baptized on this day. They wore white clothes, and so the day was called White (or Whit) Sunday.

Trinity Sunday

'Tri' means three. Trinity Sunday celebrates the belief that there is only one God, but he can be seen in three ways – Father, Son and Spirit. This is a complicated idea to understand, but think of water, ice and steam – the same thing in three different forms. Christians believe that God the Father is a spirit who never changes. When Jesus was alive on earth he was completely man, but also completely God. The Holy Spirit is the way God works in the world. The Trinity is therefore the way that

Christians describe God. On Trinity Sunday, Christians think about what God is like, and about their own lives as Christians.

Harvest festival

Harvest festivals are usually held in September or October. They are a time for saying 'thank you'. Christians believe that God made everything in the world, so at harvest time they thank him for providing food and all the other things that we need to live. In the days when most people were farmers, harvest festival was a time for thanking God that their crops had been safely harvested.

Churches are decorated for harvest festival

Today, harvest is more of a symbol of how much everyone depends on each other. Special church services are held for harvest festivals. Churches are beautifully decorated with lots of fruit and flowers. Often, there are things like bread and water, too, because they are necessary for life. The decorations remind people to thank God for everything.

Test yourself

When is Ascension Day?

When is Pentecost?

What do Christians believe the disciples were given at Pentecost?

What does 'Tri' mean?

When are harvest festivals held?

Think it through

1 Do you think that 'the birthday of the Church' is a good name for Pentecost? Give reasons for your answer.

2 What does Trinity Sunday celebrate? What do Christians believe are the three parts of the Trinity?

3 Make a display called 'Harvest'. You could use objects as well as writing and pictures.

Special occasions I

This section tells you about special services held when people join the Church.

Baptism

Baptism is a service when someone joins the Church and is officially given their name. Sometimes the word Christening is used instead. In most denominations, the person being baptized is a baby, but there is no age limit. Babies are brought to church by their parents. Friends or relatives who are called godparents or sponsors also take part. The parents and the godparents promise that they will bring the child up to believe in Jesus and follow his teachings.

Baptism is often part of an ordinary church service. The parents and godparents stand near the font. The font is a special basin which contains holy water. The vicar or priest uses a little of the water to make the sign of the cross on the baby's forehead. As they do this, they say 'I baptize you (baby's name) in the name of the Father, and of the Son, and of the Holy Spirit.'

Baptizing a baby

A total immersion baptism

Total immersion baptism

In the Baptist Church, babies are not baptized. Baptists think that someone being baptized should be old enough to make promises for themselves. There is a service when babies are blessed, but anyone being baptized is usually at least in their late teens. The person receives teaching about Christianity, and is then baptized by **total immersion**. This means that their whole body is put under the water. Baptists do not use a font. The person being baptized walks down some steps into a special tank of water in the floor of the church. Sometimes a local swimming pool, river or the sea is used instead. They promise that they are sorry for things they have done wrong, and that they believe in Jesus. Then their whole body is carefully tipped under the water. They usually leave the pool by a different set of steps. This is to show they are starting a new life with Jesus.

Baptism in the Orthodox Church

In the Orthodox Church, babies are baptized by total immersion, too. The priest says 'The servant of God (baby's name) is baptized into the Name of the Father, Amen. And of the Son, Amen. And of the Holy Spirit, Amen.' As each part of the Trinity is mentioned, the baby is gently immersed in the water. As soon as they have been baptized, the baby has special oil put on eight different parts of their body. This is called **Chrismation**.

Why are people baptized?

Christians believe that baptism is a ceremony that washes away sin. This does not mean just the wrong things that a person has done. It also includes all the things which put up barriers between people and God. Christians believe that baptism is the spiritual birth of the person. This is why some Christians call themselves 'born again'.

Confirmation

Confirmation is a service held by Churches which baptize babies. The confirmation service lets people make for themselves the promises that were made for them when they were babies. Each person who is going to be confirmed answers questions about what they believe, and the bishop lays his hands on their head as he prays for them. In the Roman Catholic Church, the bishop makes the sign of the cross in oil on the person's forehead. At the end of the service, the person is welcomed as a full member of the Church.

Test yourself

What is baptism?

What does total immersion mean?

What does Chrismation mean?

What is confirmation?

Think it through

1 What is total immersion baptism? Explain how it is different from other baptisms.

2 Why do Churches hold confirmation services?

3 If possible, ask a member of the local clergy to come and talk to your group about baptism. Remember to prepare some questions first!

New words

Chrismation service in which a person is anointed with oil

Confirmation service in which people make baptism promises again, for themselves

Total immersion baptism where the whole body is placed under the water

Special occasions II

This section tells you what Christians teach about marriage and death.

Marriage

Christians believe that marriage is a gift from God. He intended men and women to marry so that they can help each other. Many Christians choose to marry in church, but they do not have to. Marriage is different from all other church services, because it is a legal ceremony as well as a religious one. Some of the words of the marriage service must be included by law, because the service has to obey the law of the country. As well as the couple and the vicar, at least two other people must be present. They are called witnesses. At the end of the service, all five people must sign the register, which is a legal document.

The marriage service

The people who are getting married are called the bride and bridegroom. In the marriage service, they say that they do not know any reason why they should not marry each other. Then they promise that they will love each other and stay together until one of them dies. As a sign of the promises, they usually give each other a ring. The rings are worn on the third finger of the left hand. There are prayers asking God to look after the couple in their life together. Some wedding services end with a service of the Eucharist (see pages 20–21).

Marriage in the Orthodox Churches

In Orthodox Churches, the wedding service is in two parts. In the first part, the priest blesses rings which the couple give to each other. In the second part, the priest places crowns on the couple's heads. In Greek Churches, these are made of leaves and flowers. In Russian Churches, they are made of silver or gold. They are a symbol that God will bless the couple. At the end of the service, the couple drink from the same cup of wine. This is a symbol of the life that they will share together.

Divorce

Sometimes a couple do not stay married until one of them dies. If a marriage is ended while the husband and wife are still alive, it is called a **divorce**. Some Christians believe that divorce is wrong. Other Christians believe that a man or woman who has been divorced should be able to marry someone else if they want to. Some Churches do not allow people to marry again in church if they have been divorced.

The bride and groom exchange wedding rings

Death

Christians believe that death is not the end of a person. They believe that the body is left behind, and a person's **soul** continues life with God. So a Christian funeral is a time of hope as well as sadness. A funeral includes prayers for the person who has died, and for their family and friends. There are hymns, and usually a talk which remembers what the person was like when they were alive.

A funeral service in a Roman Catholic church

After death

Belief in life after death is an important part of Christian teaching, but there are no fixed ideas about what it is like. Christians believe that the soul lives on and that death is a new beginning in their life with God. Most Churches teach about a time at the end of the world when Jesus will return as King to judge everyone, living and dead.

Test yourself

Why is marriage different from other church services?

What are the crowns made of in Orthodox weddings?

What is divorce?

What is a funeral?

What is a soul?

Think it through

1 Why do you think that getting married in church is important for many Christians?

2 Do you think it is right for people who have been divorced to marry again in church? Give reasons.

3 Why is a Christian funeral a time of hope as well as sadness? What do you think should be included in the talk at someone's funeral?

New words

Divorce ending of a marriage while the husband and wife are still alive
Soul a person's spirit which lives on after their body has died

Glossary

Altar special table used for the service of Holy Communion page 11

Angel messenger of God page 24

Anoint to rub with oil page 27

Apostle early Christian preacher page 22

Baptism special service for people who are joining the church page 16

Bishops senior vicars page 12

Carols joyful songs page 38

Cathedrals important churches page 14

Chalice special cup used in Eucharist services page 20

Chrismation service in which a person is anointed with oil page 45

Christ God's chosen one page 6

Church a group of Christians (also the building where Christians meet) page 8

Confessions saying what you have done wrong page 9

Confirmation service in which people make baptism promises again, for themselves page 45

Crucify to kill someone by fastening them to a cross page 6

Denominations branches of Christianity page 12

Disciples special friends of Jesus page 26

Divorce ending of a marriage while the husband and wife are still alive page 46

Dome roof shaped like half a ball page 15

Eucharist 'thanksgiving' – important Christian service pages 20–21

Fast go without food and drink for religious reasons page 21

Gospels parts of the New Testament which tell of the life of Jesus page 22

Holy Communion most important Christian service page 16

Hymns special songs used in worship page 18

Icons pictures used in worship page 11

Judaism religion of the Jews page 22

Lord's Prayer 'Our Father' – prayer which Christians believe Jesus taught to his friends page 18

Meditate to think deeply, especially about religion page 36

Ministry Jesus' preaching and teaching page 26

Miracles amazing events which show God's power page 30

Missionary someone who travels to preach page 37

Monks men who dedicate their life to God page 34

Nuns women who dedicate their life to God page 36

Order group of monks or nuns who live by the same rules page 34

Parable story with a special meaning page 28

Parish local area page 12

Patron saints saints with a special interest in a country or situation page 34

Pilgrimage journey made for religious reasons page 35

Pope head of the Roman Catholic Church page 8

Preachers people who teach others about religion page 22

Priest someone set apart to lead worship page 9

Resurrection coming back to life page 7

Rosary beads string of beads used as a reminder of prayers page 8

Sacraments a number of services in which Christians believe they are especially blessed page 18

Saints people who were very close to God when they were alive page 8

Sermon talk which teaches about religion page 17

Services Christian meetings for worship page 11

Sins wrong-doings page 6

Soul a person's spirit which lives on after their body has died page 47

Spire pointed part of a church roof page 15

Spirit a being who is alive but does not have a body page 6

Symbols things which stand for something else page 7

Total immersion baptism where the whole body is placed under the water page 44

Vicars Anglican priests page 12

Vision dream which includes a religious experience page 32

Vows solemn promises page 36

Worship show respect and love for God page 8